The Best Edmonton Oilers Joke Book Ever

Copyright

Version 1
Copyright © 2013
Willie Harper
All rights reserved.

ISBN: 978-1-304-12126-4

Unofficial and unauthorized

This book is a joke book, written in a light hearted way.

No offence is meant to any person or group of people

Read, laugh and enjoy a joke

Introduction

Thank you for taking the time to read "The Best Edmonton Oilers Joke Book Ever". In this book we take a light hearted look at hockey and our rivals.

We have spoken with fans around the country to find the best and funniest jokes; most jokes were thought up during the game or shared in the bar after a game and a few beers.

This book covers some of the best jokes; no joke has been kept out of this book for being politically incorrect or too rude.

Get ready to share a laugh at our rival's expense …

What's the difference between the Blue Jackets goalie and a taxi driver?

A taxi driver will only let in four at a time

What do you get when you combine 20 Flames with 20 lesbians?

Forty people that don't do dick

What is the difference between a Kings fan and a pot hole?

I would swerve to avoid the pot hole

What song do Red Wings fans sing before the end of a game?

Nobody knows, there's never any of them left

What's the difference between the Blue Jackets and a mosquito?

A mosquito stops sucking

What do the Blue Jackets and lawn furniture have in common?

They both fold and end up in the cellar at the end of the season

Did you hear the Blue Jackets are moving to the Philippines?

They are going to be called the Manilla Folders

What do I have in common with the Jets?

We'll both be watching the Stanley Cup on television

What is a Flames fan's favorite whine?

"We can't beat the Oilers"

Why did BP hire the Blue Jackets to clean up the Gulf oil spill?

Because they'll go out there and throw in the towel

How do you get a Canucks fans eyes to light up?

Shine a flashlight in his ears

What's the difference between Bigfoot and a smart Canucks fan?

Bigfoot has been sighted before

How do you make a Flames fan laugh on Monday?
Tell them a joke on Friday

How do you get four Kings fans to sit on a stool?
Turn it upside down

Albert Einstein is at a party and he's surrounded by a small crowd of admirers. He introduces himself to the first member of the group, and asks, "What is your IQ?"
The man answers, "191."

"Wonderful!" says Einstein. "We will talk about the Grand Unification Theory and the mysteries of the universe. We will have much to discuss!"

Albert then turns to a woman and asks, "What's your IQ?" She responds, "123."

"Ah!" says Albert. "We can discuss politics and current affairs. We, too, have much to discuss!"

Einstein then notices a third member of the group and again inquires about the man's IQ.

This time the answer is "62." The great physicist ponders for a moment, then brightens and says, "Go Wings"

A father and son are in line ready to watch the game, and the young son is asking his father to buy him a "Flames Suck" T-shirt. The father hesitates, but finally tells his son, "You can have the shirt if you promise never to say that word"

"That's right," says the T-shirt vendor, wanting to make the sale. "'Suck' isn't a very nice word."

"No," replies the father. "I meant the word 'Flames'."

Four hockey fans, an Oilers fan, a Blue Jackets fan, a Canucks fan, and a Red Wings fan are climbing a mountain and arguing about who loves his team more.

The Blue Jackets fan insists he is the most loyal. "This is for the Jackets!" he yells, and jumps off the side of the mountain.

Not to be outdone, the Canucks fan shouts, "This is for the

Nucks!" and throws himself off the mountain.

The Oilers fan is next to profess his love for his team. He yells, "This is for everyone!" and pushes the Red Wings fan off.

An Oilers fan, Canucks fan, and Red Wings fan are walking down the road. They come across a naked lady passed out on the side of the road.

So in respect they all take off their caps and cover her private parts and continue on. When the

cops eventually arrive, the officers are confused
so one cop lifts the Oilers cap off the left breast, seeing nothing unusual he puts it back.

Then he lifts the Canucks cap off the right breast, seeing nothing unusual he puts it back.

Finally he lifts the Red Wings cap, then puts it down, lifts it up and puts it down three more times until finally his partner stops him and says "Hey what's your problem? Are some sort of pervert?"

"No, I'm just confused because

it's usually an asshole under a Red Wings cap"

A teacher asks her students if they are Canucks fans.

One of them says, "No, my Dad is an Oilers fan, so is my Mom, so I'm one too"

So the teacher says, "Well, that's not very good; if your mother and father were both morons, would that make you a moron too?"

"No, that would make me a Canucks fan."

Why does Stephen King go to Blue Jackets games?
He likes horror stories

St. Peter was manning the Pearly Gates when 40 Canucks fans showed up. Never having seen a Canucks fan at heaven's door, St. Peter said he would have to check with God. After hearing the news, God instructed him to admit the 10 most virtuous from the group.

A few minutes later, Saint Peter returned to God breathless and said, "They're gone."

"What? All of the Canucks fans are gone?" asked God.

"No" replied Saint Peter "The Pearly Gates!"

What is the difference between a Flames fan and a coconut?

One's thick and hairy and the others a tropical fruit

Three old hockey fans are in a church, praying for their teams.

The first one asks, "Oh lord, when will we win the Stanley

Cup?" God replies "In five years' time"

"But I will be dead by then", said the old man.

The second fan asks "When will the Oilers win the Stanley Cup?"

"Next year", God replies

But I'll be dead by then, said the old man

The last man asks "When will the Flames win the Stanley Cup?"

God thinks and then says "I will be dead by then"

Rumor has it that to cut the cost of the repairs to the Blue Jackets scoreboard, only the lights in the half used to show the opponents score will be fixed.

The other half will just have 'Home 0' painted on in yellow emulsion.

The Blue Jackets are apparently under investigation by the IRS for tax evasion.

Apparently they have been claiming for Silver Polish for the past 10 years.

What's the difference between a female Flames fan and a bull dog?
Lipstick

There was once a fanatical Oilers fan who thought of nothing but hockey all day long. He talked about hockey, read about hockey, watched nothing but hockey on television and attended games as often as he possibly could.

Finally his poor wife could not stand it any longer. One night she said, 'I honestly believe you love the Oilers more than you love me!'

'Blimey,' said the fan, 'I love the Panthers more than I love you!'

I've started watching the Jets, as my doctor says I should avoid any excitement.

Top tip for Red Wings fans; don't waste money on expensive new jerseys every season.

Simply strap a large inflatable penis to your forehead, and

everyone will immediately know which team you support.

One of the highest paid players in the NHL, John had everything going for him. He had a fancy new house, an expensive new sports car, lots of designer clothes.

His only problem was that he had three girlfriends and he couldn't decide which one to marry. So he decided to give $10,000 to each woman to see what she would do with it.

The first woman bought new clothes for herself and had an expensive new haircut, a massage, facial, manicure and pedicure.

The second woman bought a top-of-the range DVD and CD player, as well as an expensive set of golf clubs and tennis racquet and gave them all to John. "I used the money to buy you these gifts because I love you," she told him.

The third woman invested the money in the stock market, and within a short time had doubled her investment. She gave John back the initial £10,000 and reinvested the profit. "I'm investing in our future because I love you so much," she said.

John considered carefully how each woman had spent the money, and then married the woman with the biggest breasts.

A Blue Jackets player had a particularly bad season and announced that he was retiring from professional hockey. In a television interview he was asked his reasons for quitting.

'Well, basically,' he said, 'it's a question of illness and fatigue.'

'Can you be more specific?' asked the interviewer.

'Well,' said the player, 'specifically the fans are sick and tired of me.

My wife told me last week that she'd leave me if I didn't stop spending so much time watching hockey games.

'What a shame!'

'Yes. I shall miss her'

A woman was reading a newspaper one morning and said to her husband:

'Look at this, dear. There's an article here about a man who traded his wife for a season ticket to the Oilers. You wouldn't do a thing like that, would you?'

'Of course I wouldn't!' replied her husband. 'The season's almost over!'

Snow White arrived home one evening to find her home destroyed by fire. She was especially worried because she'd left all seven dwarves asleep inside. As she scrambled among the wreckage, frantically calling their names, suddenly she heard someone shout: "The Flames will win the Stanley Cup this year"

"Thank goodness," sobbed Snow White. "At least Dopey's still alive!"

Four surgeons are taking a tea break:

1st surgeon says "Accountants are the best to operate on because when you open them up, everything inside is numbered"

2nd surgeon says "Nope, librarians are the best. Everything inside them is in alphabetical order"

3rd surgeon says "Well you should try electricians. Everything inside them is color coded"

4th surgeon says "I prefer Flames fans. They're heartless, spineless, gutless and their heads and asses are interchangeable"

How do you change a Kings fans mind?

Blow in his ear!

What's the difference between a Flames fan and a broken clock?

Even a broken clock is right twice a day

What's the difference between a Jets fan and a coconut?

You can get a drink out of a coconut

Two men were walking through a cemetery when they see a tombstone that read: "Here lies John Burn, a good man and a Flames fan"

So, one of them asked the other: "When the hell did they start putting two people in one grave?"

Two Canucks fans jump off a cliff. Which one hits the ground first?

Who gives a F**k!

What do you get when you cross a Canucks fan with a pig?

I don't know, there are some things a pig just won't do

What do you call a Red Wings fan on the moon?

A Problem

What do you call 100 Wings fans on the moon?

An even bigger problem

What do you call all the Wings fans on the moon?

Problem solved

How do you define 199 Canucks fans?

Gross Stupidity

Why do Canucks fans whistle whilst sitting on the toilet?

So they know which end to wipe

What's the difference between a Red Wings fan and an Onion?

No one cries when you chop up a Red Wings fan

Did you hear that Postal Service has just recalled their latest stamps?

They had images of Maple Leafs players on them, people couldn't figure out which side to spit on

How many Red Wings fans does it take to pave up a driveway?

Depends how thin you slice them

What would you call a pregnant Flames fan?

A dope carrier

What do you call a Canucks fan with half a brain?

Gifted

What do Flames fans use as birth control?

Their personalities

How many Red Wings fans does it take to stop a moving Bus?

Never enough

What do you call a Canucks fan with no arms and legs?

Trustworthy

What's the difference between a dead dog in the road and a dead Jets fan?

Skid marks in front of the dog

What's the difference between a Canucks fan and a Vibrator?

A Canucks fan is a real dick

If you see a Red Wings fan on a bicycle, why should you never swerve and hit him?

You don't want to damage your bike

Sadly the homes of the whole Blue Jackets team were broken into last night. The entire contents of each of their trophy cabinets were stolen.

The cops are believed to be looking for a man with a number of pieces of green felt

What would you call two Canucks fans going over a cliff in an SUV?

A complete waste of space. You could have squeezed six of them into one of those

There's a rumor that after the current sponsorship expires, the Blue Jackets have lined up a new sponsor, Tampax

The owners thought it was an appropriate change as the team is going through a very bad period

What's the difference between a Canucks fan and a bucket of crap?

The bucket

How do you get a one armed Red Wings fan down from a tree?

Wave at him

How do you keep a Canucks fan busy?

Put him in a round room and tell him to sit in the corner

What do Kings fans and mushrooms have in common?

They both sit in the dark and feed on nothing but crap

How many Canucks fans does it take to change a light bulb?

It doesn't matter, because they're all condemned to eternal darkness anyway

Todd Richards was going to the Blue Jackets Halloween party dressed as a pumpkin

But at midnight he still hadn't turned into a coach

Max Lapierre walks into a bar with a pile of dog crap in his hand and says to the bartender

'Look what I nearly trod in!'

How is a pint of milk different than a Flames fan?

If you leave the milk out for a week it develops a culture

What's the difference between a Canucks fan and a sperm?

At least a sperm has one chance in 5 million of becoming a human being

There's a rumor going about that if you buy a season ticket at the Joe Louis Arena then you get a free space suit. Apparently it's due to the lack of atmosphere

How do you save a Canucks fan from drowning?

Take your foot off his head

What's the difference between the Joe Louis Arena and a Hedgehog?

On a hedgehog, the pricks are on the outside

What do hemorrhoids and Red Wings fans have in common?

They're both a complete pain in the ass and never seem to go away completely

Why did the Canucks fan climb the glass window?

To see what was on the other side

What's the difference between a Red Wings fan and a Chimp?

One's hairy, stupid and smells, and the other is a chimpanzee

An anxious woman goes to her doctor. "Doctor," she asks nervously, "I'm a bit worried - can you get pregnant from anal intercourse?"

"Of course," replies the doctor, "Where do you think Red Wings fans come from?"

How do you kill a Canucks fan when he's been drinking?

Slam the toilet seat on his head

What's the difference between Pamela Anderson and the Blue Jackets goalie?

Pam's only got two tits in front of her

Santa Claus, the tooth fairy, an intelligent Canucks fan and an old bum are walking down the street together when they all spot a fifty dollar bill on the sidewalk. Who gets it?

The old bum of course, as the other three are mythical creatures

How can you tell a level headed Canucks fan?

He dribbles from both sides of his mouth at the same time

What do you get if you cross a Red Wings fan with a pig?

Thick bacon

Burglars broke into the home of a Flames fan and stole two books.

"The thing that upsets me", he said "is that I hadn't finished coloring them in yet"

What do you get if you cross a Monkey with a Canucks fan?

Nothing, monkeys are far too clever to screw one of their fans.

What is the difference between a battery and a Blue Jackets fan?

A battery has a positive side

Why do Canucks fans have moustaches?

So they can look like their mothers

What do Red Wings fans and laxatives have in common?

They both irritate the crap out of you

What's the ideal weight for a Flames fan?

Three pounds, that's including the Urn

Two Red Wings fans are on the plane on the way to a game

One turns to the other and says "Hey John! If this plane turns upside-down will we fall out?"

"No way Steve, of course we'll still be pals!"

You're trapped in a room with a Lion, a snake and a Canucks fan. You have a gun with two bullets. What should you do?

Shoot the Canucks fan, twice

What do you call a Canucks fan in a suit?

The Defendant

Why did God make Red Wings fans smelly?

So blind people could laugh at them too

What do you call 100 Red Wings fans at the bottom of a cliff?

A good start

What do you call a dead Canucks fan found in a closet?

Last year's winner of the hide and seek contest

What do you call a Canucks fan that does well on an IQ test?

A cheat

What has 40,000 arms and an IQ of 170

The Joe Louis Arena at every home game

Why do people take an instant dislike to Red Wings fans?

It saves time

What do you call twenty Red Wings fans sky diving?

Diarrhea

What's clear and goes on a prick? A clear condom

What's black and goes on a prick? A black condom

What's red, white and goes on a prick? A Red Wings Jersey

A woman has pleaded guilty to stalking a number of the Blue Jackets players. She has been sentenced to three years' probation, told to attend counseling, and encouraged to set her sights a little bit higher.

What do you say to a Red Wings fan with a job?

Can I have a Big Mac please

What do you get if you see a Canucks fan buried up to his neck in sand?

More sand

What's the difference between a Canucks fan and a shopping cart?

The shopping cart has a mind of its own

A Red Wings fan goes to his doctor to find out what's wrong with him.

"Your problem is you're fat" says the doctor

"I'd like a second opinion" responds the man

"OK, you're ugly too" replies the doctor

A man walks into an antique shop and sees an ornamental brass rat. He thinks "that'll be perfect for his Mother's birthday", so he asks the store owner how much it is.

"$25 for the rat, $100 for the story", replies the man.

"Forget the story" says the man, so buys the rat for $25. He walks off down the street, but has not gone 30 yards when a rat comes up from the gutter and starts to follow him. Soon more arrive, and in a few minutes the whole street is a sea of rats, all following him. He keeps walking until he comes to a cliff, then he throws the brass rat over the edge, and thousands of rats follow, one after each other, plunging to certain death. The man then runs back to the store.

"Ah", says the store owner, "you'll be back for the story"

"Screw the story; do you have a brass Flames fan?"

What do you call a 350 pound Jets fan?

An anorexic

What do you call a Flames fan holding a bottle of champagne after the Stanley Cup?

A waiter

How many Blue Jackets players does it take to win the Stanley Cup?

Nobody knows and we may never find out

The ASPCA have acted swiftly after recent results.

If you see any Blue Jackets fans walking a dog please call them immediately, as they're not very good at holding on to leads

A truck driver used to keep himself amused by scaring every Red Wings fan he saw walking down the Street in their jersey. He would swerve as if to hit them, and at the last minute, swerve back onto the road.

One day as he was driving along the road, he saw a priest hitch-hiking. He thought he would do his good deed for the day and offer the priest a lift.

"Where are you going, Father'?" he asked.

"I'm going to say mass"

"No problem," said the driver, "Jump in and I'll give you a ride"

The priest climbed into the truck and they set off down the road. Suddenly the driver sees a Red Wings fan on the sidewalk, and instinctively swerved as if to hit him, but just in time, remembering the priest in his truck, swerved back to the road again, narrowly missing him.

Although he was certain that he didn't hit him, he still heard a loud "Thud". Not understanding where the noise came from, he glanced in his mirrors, and, seeing nothing, said to the priest, "Oh sorry Father, I nearly hit that Wings fan"

"No need to apologize Son," replied Father, "I got the ba*tard with the door!"

What's the difference between OJ Simpson and the Blue Jackets?

OJ at least had a defense

What's the difference between a vacuum cleaner and the Canucks?

There's only one dirt bag in a vacuum cleaner

What did the Flames fan say after his team won the Stanley Cup?

"Dammit mom, why'd you wake me up? I was having an amazing dream!"

What do the Blue Jackets and possums have in common?

Both play dead at home and get killed on the road

What is the difference between a Red Wings fan and a baby?

The baby will stop whining after a while

How many Canucks players does it take to change a tire?

One, unless it's a blowout, in which case they all show up

What do the Blue Jackets and Billy Graham have in common?

They both can make 13,000 people stand up and yell "Jesus Christ"

How do you stop a Jets fan from beating his wife?

Dress her in an Oilers Jersey

How do you castrate a Canucks fan?

Kick his sister in the mouth

What should you do if you find three Canucks fans buried up to their neck in cement?

Get more cement

What's the difference between a Red Wings fan and a carp?

One is a bottom-feeding, scum sucker, and the other is a fish

How did the Stars fan die from drinking milk?

The cow fell on him

What does a Flames fan do when his team wins the Stanley Cup?

He turns off the PlayStation

Did you hear that the Blue Jackets don't have a website?

They can't string three "W's" together

What does a Flames fan and a bottle of beer have in common?

They're both empty from the neck up

Why do Canucks fans keep their caps on their dashboards?

So they can park in handicap spaces

How do you keep a Kings fan from masturbating?

You paint his dick in Oilers colors and he won't beat it for years

Why do the Blue Jackets want to change their name to the Columbus Tampons?

Because they are only good for one period

What do the Dallas Stars and the movie Broke Back Mountain have in common?

They both have cowboys that suck

Why doesn't Syracuse have a professional hockey team?

Because then New York would want one

Why was Todd Richards mad when the Blue Jackets playbook was stolen?

Because he hadn't finished coloring it in

What has 400 feet; is smelly and has 3 teeth?

The front row at a Canucks game

What's the difference between a hockey game and wrestling?

In a hockey game, the fights are real

What do the Canucks and the Titanic have in common?

They both look good until they hit the ice

What's the difference between Frequent Flyer Miles and the Blue Jackets?

Frequent Flyer Miles earn points

Why did the Canucks enforcer retire early?

He was ice fishing and got run over by the Zamboni

Why don't the Blue Jackets drink tea?

Because they don't have any cups

What do you call five Red Wings players standing ear to ear?

A wind tunnel

Why are the Blue Jackets like grizzly bears?

Every fall they go into hibernation

What does a recent high school dropout and the Blue Jackets have in common?

They're both young, have no goals and no good prospects

What's the difference between a fat chick and the Blue Jackets?

Even a fat chick scores every once in a while

Why do the Blue Jackets suck at geometry?

Because they never have any points

What is it called when a Red Wings player blows in another Wings players ear?

Data transfer

What's blue and red and goes down the toilet faster than Liquid Plumber?

The Columbus Blue Jackets

What do a fine wine and the Canucks have in common?

They both spend a lot of time in the cellar, cost too much and are only enjoyed on select occasions.

What's the difference between the Nationwide Arena and a red light district?

In a red light district, you pay $200 bucks and somebody scores

Why are the Canucks like the Canada Post?

They both wear uniforms and don't deliver

Two Canucks players were driving through the country to go bear hunting. They came upon a fork in the road where a sign read "Bear Left" so they went home.

The Blue Jackets have a new coach from North Korea.
Win Sum Soon

What's the difference between the Blue Jackets and a cigarette vending machine?

The vending machine has Players

How do Red Wings hockey players brain cells die?

Alone

Why do Red Wings players drive BMWs?

Because they can spell it

Why do Flames players have TGIF on their skates?

Toes Go In First

What do a criminal court judge and the coach of the Blue Jackets have in common?

They both sit behind a bench, watch an endless parade of losers go by, and wonder if they are actually making a difference.

What do the Blue Jackets team and a pace car have in common?

They both go around in circles, aren't involved in the race and are passed by all the competitors.

What do college students and the Blue Jackets have in common?

They've both finished their year by April

What's the difference between the Canucks and a bra?
A bra has two cups

Made in the USA
Middletown, DE
19 March 2019